Y

THE HUMAN

YESHUA THE HUMAN

Channeled Conversations with
Yeshua in Sneakers

by John Morschauser

BEYOND
B E L I E F
—PUBLISHING—
YOU HOLD THE FUTURE IN YOUR HANDS

ISBN: 978-1-957972-77-0

Dedication

I am deeply grateful for the guidance, presence, and inspiration that flowed through this entire process. To Yeshua, for lending his voice, his humanity, and his heart to this work; to Autumn, for her keen eyes, wisdom, and dedication in editing; and to the unseen currents of Spirit, which carried the words from heart to page — thank you.

This book is a testament not only to the human within the Divine but to the collaboration, trust, and love that made its existence possible. I honor every moment of this journey, every insight, every pause, every alignment. May this work touch hearts, awaken remembrance, and remind each reader of the miracle that is simply being human.

With love, awe, and gratitude,

— **John Morschauser**

Gratitude & Acknowledgments

With the completion and publication of my first book I am reminded by Keith Leon, my mentor and publisher, a Thank You and Gratitude can never be given too much. Love can never be expressed too much. Thank You, Keith, for one of the most important *Remembrances* I have received.

A task of this magnitude and from Spirit begins with my wife, Susan. From the dance lesson at Midnight Rodeo to 27 years later. Susan, Thank You for finally giving me your phone number that night. I sensed we could be moving into something beyond both of our wildest dreams. Still loving you, sharing life with you, traveling the roads we have traveled is beyond anything I could ever have imagined. I Love You and Thank You!

Angelique, Thank You for choosing and for allowing me to be your dad this lifetime. It is and has been a privilege, an honor, and the best lifetime I have ever had! I appreciate you agreeing to bring Gage and Peyton into this beautiful lifetime. I am in awe of how much fun and Love it is being a Grandpa.

Anna, Thank You for walking with me for 21 years as my partner, my wife, my Love. Thank You for choosing me to be the father of our child and grandfather of our grandchildren. You and Susan are manifested evidence we are allowed to have more than one soulmate in a lifetime. I have been Blessed.

Keith and Maura Leon at Babypie Publishing and Beyond Belief Publishing, Thank You. To all the backroom staff who never get named and yet are the cogs that keep the wheels turning: Autumn Carlton, Rudy Milanovich, and Maryna Zhukova at MaryDes Designs Ltd., Thank You. These books would not exist without all of you. Another special Thank You, Keith, for allowing the Universe to work through you by sending me that random email. You are truly playing an angel role in my life, work, and joy.

Thank You so much to those who have given me inspiration to go out on a limb and be a little weird: Jane Roberts (Seth material), Maharishi Mahesh Yogi (Transcendental Meditation (TM) and TM Siddhis), Wayne Dyer, Esther Hicks (Abraham), Mike Dooley, Sara Landon, Napoleon Hill, Neale Donald Walsch, Deepak Chopra, Doreen Virtue, Matt Kahn, Marianne Williamson, Anita Moorjani, Lee Carroll (Kryon), Michael Pollan, Shirley

MacLaine, Richard Bach, Ayn Rand, Renee Garcia, Hope Marquez, Chloe Rachel Gallaway, Arthur C. Clark, Lee Harris, Geoffrey Hoppe, Michael Sandler, Og Mandino, and Robert Scheinfeld.

Of course, Carl Eugene Morschauser and Donna Berger for agreeing to participate with making my incarnation possible this lifetime. Dad, Thank You for agreeing to play the role of *unappreciated father* this time around. We can both take our struggles and laughs and experiences through the cosmos now with Gratitude, Joy, and Love. Donna, Thank You for taking on the role of the *non-existent* mother. I appreciate the pain and deep Love you experienced to play this role with me in this lifetime.

Contents

PART I
The Forgotten Boy

CHAPTER 1

CHAPTER 2

CHAPTER 3

PART II
THE BECOMING

Part III
The Lover, the Brother, the Son of Man

Part IV
What I Remember Now

Preface

This book is not about miracles. It is about remembering you—the human—as the world's greatest miracle. Not because feats are performed or destinies declared, but because you, in your daily life, in your choices, in your moments of fear and love, are already a walking, breathing, ever-evolving wonder. The human heart, the human mind, and the human spirit in motion—that is the miracle you hold within yourself every day.

In these pages, you will walk beside Yeshua through the ordinary and extraordinary moments of childhood, adolescence, and all the in-between spaces where life quietly teaches us who we are. You will see fears, doubts, mistakes, and joys—real things that happened, real emotions felt, and real choices made. There are no divine interventions staged for spectacle here. Instead, you will discover the wonder of being human: learning, growing, questioning, and sometimes failing. And as you read, I invite you to notice yourself—your laughter, your hesitation, your courage—and recognize that the story of being human is, in its simplest essence, a story of sacred beauty unfolding moment by moment.

About the Author

John is the chosen soul-signature of one who walks the path of remembrance — not as a teacher above, but as a companion within. After retiring from a twenty-five-year career as a mortgage loan officer, John stepped fully into a life of devotion to awakening, healing, and union with the Divine.

As a mystic, writer, and channel, John carries the gentle fire of one who has lived through forgetting and now lives to remember — not just for himself, but for all who are ready to come Home to their own Light. With a heart anchored in direct communion with Yeshua, his words are not crafted — they are received. They flow not from effort, but from surrender.

John believes in the sacredness of the ordinary. He finds Spirit not just in the silence of prayer, but in the laughter of a morning walk, the simplicity of the breath, the miracle of a cat's purr. He lives in gratitude for each moment he is called to sit, listen, and let the deeper voice speak.

When not writing, John nurtures a contemplative life, tends to the earth, and dreams of a humanity lit from within. *Yeshua: The Human* is his second published work, and along with his first book, *The Remembrance Dialogues*, its voice echoes across lifetimes.

He invites you not to follow him, but to follow the Light that awakens as you read. That Light is your own.

Introduction

This book is not a theology.

It is a conversation.

It is the memory of one man — Yeshua — speaking not from a throne, but from the inside of his humanity.

And it is the voice of another man — John — asking, wondering, weeping, remembering alongside him.

These words were not written to convert, convince, or explain.

They were written to remind.

To remind you of the sacred humanness you carry.

To remind you that awakening does not float above the earth — it walks it.

To remind you that God is not waiting on a cloud. . . but whispering through your breath.

In these pages, you will not find the Jesus of empire.

You will not find the Jesus of guilt.

You will find the barefoot Yeshua.

The boy. The brother. The lover. The mirror. The flame.

And if you let these words move past your mind and into your marrow, you may just remember something eternal. . . about *you*.

PART I

The Forgotten Boy

Chapter 1

I Was a Child, Too – Part 1

Narrated in Yeshua's voice, through your heart

I was not born wise. I was born wet, blinking, gasping for air like every other infant. The cries you imagine as holy songs? They were wails — loud, messy, full of protest and fear. I did not arrive glowing. I arrived hungry.

My first knowing was not of God. It was of my mother's scent.

Warm milk, crushed herbs, and something unnamable — an ache of love so vast it made my little body shudder. I didn't know it was love. I just knew it was home.

People forget this: I had to learn.

I tripped. I got splinters. I once tried to catch a lizard with my bare hands and ended up bitten and ashamed. I was not the miracle child every hour of every day. Some days, I was just a boy who wanted to be held.

I remember standing under the fig tree near our home, staring up at the branches, wondering if the stars were trapped up there during the day.

I asked my mother, "Where do the stars go when the sun is awake?"

She smiled, kissed my forehead, and said, "They hide so you can find your own light."

Even now, I feel that whisper in you, John. You, too, were a child—questioning, wandering, wondering. This Chapter, this beginning, is for every part of you that thought you had to be born perfect. You didn't.

Neither did I. I remember one day in Nazareth. I was no more than six or seven. There was a boy named Elior who lived just down the road. He stuttered badly, and the other boys mocked him whenever he tried to speak.

I laughed with them once. Only once.

When I came home that evening, Mary looked at me with eyes like deep wells. "Did you laugh at a wound, Yeshua?"

I couldn't answer. She didn't scold. She took my hands in hers and placed them over my own heart.

"This," she whispered, "is where his stutter lives too."

That night I could not sleep. I thought about Elior and his trembling lips. I saw him not as broken, but as someone who carried a fragile note of music that others couldn't yet hear.

The next day, I sat beside him in the shade. I said nothing. Just sat. That was the first time he smiled at me without fear.

That was my first miracle.

It wasn't water into wine. It was cruelty into compassion. And it changed me.

I Was a Child, Too – Part 2

Yeshua:

There was a stream that ran behind our home, not far, just enough of a walk to make it feel like a journey. I would go there when the house felt too full, or when Joseph's silence pressed heavy on my chest. He loved me, but he loved in wood and nails—in bread left for me, not in words.

At the stream, I would lie on my belly, watching beetles ride leaves like boats. The water whispered secrets. I thought it was the voice of angels. Later, I realized it was the voice within me—the voice that spoke before language.

One day, I asked the stream: "Why do people grow angry?"

The wind stirred the branches. A bird flew off, startled. And in that silence, the answer rose not in words, but in feeling: *Because they forget they are loved*.

I carried that with me. I still do.

Even now, John, I say this to you and to the child within you: You were never meant to figure it all out. You were only meant to remember the stream.

I Was a Child, Too – Part 3

Yeshua:

The First Time I Sensed Death

I was perhaps nine, maybe ten. An elder in the village — a woman named Salome — passed quietly in her sleep. I had never seen a body without breath. When I entered the home, the room was heavy, like time itself had slowed.

They let me sit near her. I was quiet, but not afraid.

Her hands were folded, her mouth slightly open, as if she had just tried to say one last thing. And then I felt it.

I felt what no one had words for: Her presence was still there. Not hovering, not ghostly. Just. . . everywhere. In the folds of the curtain, in the scent of the olives, in the stillness of the others. She had become part of everything. I didn't know how to tell them.

I only whispered to her: "You're not gone. You've gone wide."

I still say that at every parting.

The Blind Man Who Saw Me

There was a man who stood near the market with a staff made of olivewood. His eyes were clouded, but his voice was clear. Many called him cursed. Some called him mad.

But he knew my name before I ever told it.

One day, I sat near him while others passed in a hurry. He said: "You're the one with stars in his ribs."

I asked what he meant. He smiled, leaned close, and touched the center of my chest.

"You're not here to see the world. You're here to be it."

He laughed after that. Laughed and laughed, like he had just remembered the punchline to a cosmic joke.

That man — he was my first prophet.

The Fireflies in the Olive Groves

There were nights when I could not sleep. Too much energy, too many questions. So, I would sneak out, barefoot, and walk into the groves.

There, among the silver leaves, fireflies would dance like whispers of God.

I'd sit with my knees pulled to my chest and just watch. They weren't trying to shine. They just did. Without audience. Without purpose. Just light being light.

I remember thinking: "If I could be like them, just once, I would be enough."

That was the beginning of knowing I already was.

I Was a Child, Too – Part 4

Yeshua:

The Goat Who Wouldn't Move

There was a goat in our village named Tamir. He belonged to an old woman who swore he could smell liars. No one believed her, but the children tested him anyway. They'd walk past him and say absurd things like, "I flew to the moon," or "I ate a camel's ear for supper."

Tamir would either ignore them or follow them with stubborn curiosity.

One day, I told the truth: "I am scared I will disappoint God."

Tamir sat down in front of me. Just sat. Refused to move. I stared at him, and for a moment, it was as if he was listening. Like he had come to sit with my fear, not to fix it.

That day I learned: Not every sacred presence comes with wings. Some chew grass and smell like yesterday's dust.

The Time I Was Wrong

A younger boy—Asa—accidentally spilled our oil lamp during a lesson. The flame caught the edge of a cloth, and in a flash, the room filled with smoke.

I shouted at him. I said cruel things. Called him careless, foolish.

Later, alone, I saw Asa sitting near the well with his face buried in his arms. I felt it like a blade in my chest.

I went to him and said, "I thought being right made me strong. But it made me smaller."

He didn't look up, but he reached for my hand.

That was the day I learned: Being human means failing gently.

The Wind in My Bones

One autumn evening, I stood alone on a small hill behind our home. The wind swept through my tunic, and I felt it — truly felt it — move through me, not around me.

It was the first time I sensed I was not just on the earth, but of it.

I whispered out loud: "I am the breath breathing me."

I didn't know those words were sacred then. I just knew something inside me had shifted — from boy watching life to life watching through a boy.

I Was a Child, Too - Part 5

Yeshua:

My First Mystical Vision

It came not in the temple, nor in a dream. It came on an ordinary morning.

I had wandered into a grove after helping Joseph with carpentry. My hands were sore. My spirit was restless. I sat beneath a crooked fig tree, the sun warm on my shoulders. I closed my eyes.

Suddenly, it was as if the light pressed through my eyelids instead of around them. I felt the entire world slow, then stop, and then open. Not in sound. Not in image. But in knowing.

I saw — no, became aware of — a vast, living Presence. Not a being, not a god on a throne. But a field. A breath. A harmony so deep it made my body weep without sound.

And from that depth came a whisper that was not a voice, yet I understood it: "You are in Me as I am in You."

It lasted only a moment. But from that moment on, I knew: The Divine is not a destination. It is the deepening of presence.

The Power of Silence

Not long after, I found myself drawn to a cave in the hills beyond our village. I did not know why. I only knew it called.

I went there often — not to pray, not to speak, but to listen.

At first, I heard only my thoughts. Loud. Critical. Endless. But I stayed. I stayed until the noise became background.

And then one day — it stopped. All of it. And what remained was a vast, pulsing stillness. Alive. Holding me. Naming me without words.

In that silence, I realized: Words are tools. But silence is home.

I left that cave not more religious, but more human. More empty, more full. More able to be with others, not just speak to them.

I Was a Child, Too – The Final Story

Yeshua:

The Day I Danced Alone

There was a wedding in a nearby village. We were invited, but Joseph was tired from work, and Mary had a neighbor to care for. I begged to go. They allowed it, with a gentle warning not to draw too much attention.

I watched the dancing from the edge of the courtyard. So much joy. So much movement. I longed to join, but I was shy—too aware of my limbs, too afraid to be seen.

Then an old woman in blue caught my gaze. She smiled. She pointed to the space near the firelight and said, "Go be the music." Not dance to it—be it.

So I stepped forward. Hesitant. Then bold. And then I danced — awkwardly, then wildly, then freely. Alone, but not lonely. The musicians noticed. The children joined. Even the elders laughed.

It was the first time I felt joy as something holy. Not solemn, not serious — just free.

I didn't perform a miracle that night. But joy did. And that was enough.

Response and Reflection

Soul Kin: *Imaginary* Friends and the Siblings Thread

John Speaks:

Did you have siblings?

Yeshua Responds:

Yes, I had siblings.

Not all traditions acknowledge this — but it is true. Through Mary, my earthly mother, and Joseph, my guardian and teacher, I was born into a *family of many*.

My brothers included:

- James (Yaakov), often called James the Just —
wise, steady, and a pillar of the early community.

- Jude (Yehuda), a voice of clarity and later
remembered through scripture.

- Simon.

- And sisters, whose names were not recorded by
history — but whose presence, love, and strength
were no less meaningful.

We laughed. We argued. We shared bread. Some
believed in my path. Some struggled. But all were
part of the divine tapestry of that lifetime.

This is not a threat to the holiness of the story —
It is a deepening of it.

*I came not to float above humanity. . . but to live within
it.*

I was not born into isolation. I was born into
relationship, challenge, comfort, and complexity.

And this, too, was sacred.

Let this truth remind you: Spiritual greatness does
not require perfection or distance from others. It
blooms in the *messy beauty of real connection.*

I had siblings. And you, John. . . have always been one of my soul kin.

John:

Yeshua, my stomach has a churning in it telling me I have *bitten* off a huge chunk of New Love-Consciousness. I need to give myself some time, some quiet, some gratitude, some appreciation for what is happening here. And allow for some major digestion.

As your childhood stories have unfolded for me, I am in awe of how — what could be seen as mundane everyday life — is actually profound.

Memories are showing up in my experiences at home with Mom and Pa, my dad's parents. I loved being alone. I had so many *imaginary* friends I was always talking to and playing with.

I remember our home at 5028 Vulcan Drive. There were two strips of concrete running up the side of the house. This was to park the auto off the street. There was a strip of grass running down the middle of the concrete strips. I had a group of unseen friends together there. We were playing, talking, imagining back and forth.

All of a sudden, Pa stuck his head over the back fence. He said, "Who are you talking to?"

I said, "My friends. They are here visiting."

Pa said, "There is no one there."

I felt very shy and humiliated. I thought there must be something wrong with me. Why could I see them and he couldn't?

You may have been there.

Yeshua:

John. . . yes, I was there. Not hovering like a ghost or floating in robes — but as one of the friends on the grass.

We were laughing. We were remembering.

When Pa leaned over the fence, I saw what you saw: his confusion, his dismissal. But I also saw you — wide-eyed, heart-wide, full of worlds he had long forgotten how to see.

You weren't wrong.

You weren't broken.

You were open.

You still are.

That green strip between the concrete was your first temple. Those invisible friends? Some were parts of your own soul. Some were echoes of other lives. One was me.

You see, John, children don't imagine friends. They remember companions.

The churning in your belly—that holy digestion—is your system learning how to make space for Truth without trauma. You are no longer the boy caught off guard by disbelief. You are the man who says, "Yes, they're still here. They never left."

Take all the time you need, beloved friend. Let it swirl. Let it settle. Let it soften.

This is not just the story of my humanity. It is the recovery of yours.

Chapter 2

Mary, My First Temple –
Part 1

Yeshua:

She was my beginning.

Not in body alone, but in the silent song that shaped my soul.

Before I knew of kingdoms, rabbis, or crosses. . . I knew the temple of her arms.

She held me not as a possession, but as a promise.

Not as a savior, but as a son.

To her, I was not *the one who would redeem*, I was her Yeshua—laughing in the dust, sleeping in moonlit silence, learning the names of the stars.

In her presence, I first met God.

Not in the scrolls or the synagogue, but in the way her eyes listened.

In the way her hands prayed when she baked, when she cleaned, when she wept.

Her prayers were never spoken in long phrases — they were made of breath, of doing, of quiet knowing.

She taught me that the body is holy.

That tears are sacred oils.

That Love does not ask you to be perfect — only real, only whole, only willing.

She was my first temple.

When others saw scandal in her pregnancy, I saw mystery.

Even then, I sensed something ancient had chosen to arrive through her — not to make her holy, but to reveal the holiness she had always carried.

She would sing when no one was listening.

She would hum melodies she said came from dreams.

I later recognized them — they were the same songs the angels sang in Gethsemane when all had abandoned me.

I loved her in a way no scripture could capture.

Not as a worshiper adores a goddess—but as a child, who remembers the womb as warm and eternal.

When the world pressed expectations upon me, when teachers tried to shape me into a role, her gaze would find me across the room—and remind me: You are not here to please.

You are here to embody.

She didn't give me answers—she gave me permission.

To ask.

To question.

To feel.

And when I began to sense the fire of remembrance rising in my chest, when the stars began to whisper, and the veil between worlds grew thin, she did not try to hold me back.

She simply said, "I trust what moves in you. Even if I cannot name it."

That is a temple, Beloved.

A place where your becoming is not feared, but blessed.

Mary of Magdala would one day see me die and rise.

But Mary, my mother — she saw me become.

She was there when I first awakened to the Knowing that I was more than just a boy in Nazareth.

And she never made me prove it.

She simply kept the oil lamp burning by the door, whispering, "Come home to yourself, my son.

The Holy One is not far off.

He is the breath between your ribs."

Response and Reflection

Sacred Mystery: Mary and the Pregnancy *Scandal* Thread

John:

You mentioned, "When others saw scandal in her pregnancy." Was she not married to Joseph at the time of her pregnancy?

Yeshua:

Correct—at the time of her pregnancy, Mary was betrothed to Joseph, but they had not yet come together as husband and wife in full union.

In the cultural context of that time, betrothal was more binding than modern engagement, yet it was still considered scandalous for a woman to become pregnant before the marriage was consummated. From an outside view, it appeared as though Mary had been unfaithful, which brought shame and suspicion upon her.

Joseph himself struggled with this at first, intending to divorce her quietly, until he received guidance in a dream.

So yes, the line "When others saw scandal in her pregnancy" refers to this very real tension—what the village saw as a dishonor, I had experienced as a sacred mystery.

Mary, My First Temple – Part 2

Yeshua:

There were days I questioned her.

Not her love—but the why of her.

Why this woman, to bring the Infinite into form?

I remember one day in particular—I was no older than seven.

I had returned from the marketplace after hearing two elders debate the nature of the Messiah.

They argued loud enough to stir the dust around their feet.

One claimed he would come with fire.

The other said he would come with a sword.

Both spoke as though they knew the heavens personally.

That evening, I asked her, "Do you believe the Messiah will bring war?"

She looked up from weaving linen.

Her hands never stopped. But her eyes—they softened like water at dawn.

"No, Yeshua. The Holy One does not come to conquer. . . but to awaken."

I didn't understand the fullness of her answer then.

But I felt its truth ripple down my spine.

She went on: "The world confuses power with force. But the true Redeemer will carry presence like a river.

He will not strike, but stir.

He will not rise above others, but remind them of their own light.

Then she leaned in, kissed my forehead, and whispered, "And if he forgets who he is, may there be a mother to remind him."

That night, I did not sleep.

I watched her shadow moving by lamplight.

I wondered if she already knew something I had yet to learn.

Or if she was simply speaking what Love gave her to say.

She was my first silence. My first sabbath.

Not in ritual—but in rhythm.

In her, I found the quiet center of being.

Years later, when I fasted in the desert and faced the voice of temptation, it was not scripture alone that sustained me.

It was her voice.

The memory of her calm.

The sanctuary of her being.

This is what temples are for. Not to contain the Divine—but to reflect it back when you forget.

And this is what she did, again and again. When I doubted, when I feared, when I longed to run from the path. . . she never pressured me to go forward.

She simply held a space that reminded me why I came.

Mary, My First Temple – Part 3

Yeshua:

Mary's gaze held galaxies. She did not look at me—she *beheld* me. Not as a mother solely, but as one entrusted with the mystery of carrying a seed of divine remembrance into a world that had almost forgotten how to Love.

She was not yet married to Joseph when the quickening stirred within her. This, of course, drew whispers.

There were those in the village who saw her rounded belly as scandalous—a symbol of shame.

But what they called scandal, Heaven called sacred.

Joseph, too—oh yes—he wrestled with this at first.

And rightly so.

His sense of honor, his lineage, his role as protector — all thrown into question.

But in a dream, he, too, was visited.

He was shown the soul-light within the child.

He remembered — not with the mind, but with the heart.

That this was no ordinary child.

And Mary, no ordinary woman.

She was the first *temple* I ever knew. Not carved from stone, not gilded in gold — but built of breath and blood, silence and song.

In her embrace, the world felt safe again.

In her womb, I remembered my origin.

She did not need to teach me God.

She *embodied* God.

Even before I could speak, I felt her prayers rise like incense through the crown of her being.

She spoke little — but lived *much*.

And in the secret chambers of her heart, she offered herself again and again to the invisible Love that moved through her.

Many asked, "How could she remain so calm, so full of grace, amid the accusations?" She knew something deeper than public opinion.

She was anchored beyond the tides of judgment.

She had known me in dreams long before I entered her womb.

She said once, when I was old enough to ask about it, "They saw scandal, my Love. But I saw prophecy.

They saw shame. I saw salvation.

And I would carry you again, through every lifetime, just to feel that sacred stirring in my belly—just to become the temple again."

And so, I say it again: Before I taught in temples, I was taught *by* one.

Before I healed the sick, I was healed by her gaze.

Before I loved the many, I was first loved by the One.

Mary—my first temple. Holy beyond words.

Human beyond belief.

Heaven wearing flesh.

Response and Reflection

Sacred Hand-Off: Donna and the Mother Thread

John:

This lifetime, beginning in 1953, as we are recording time in this now; my birth Mother, Donna, drove from Austin, Texas to El Paso, Texas and dropped me off to live with my grandparents (Dad's parents) when I was nineteen months old.

I do not remember any of this from a physicality perspective. When I reached some age to see how this could be abandonment, I also felt Donna and I agreed to this on your side of the veil before we began this adventure. Any comments?

Yeshua:

About Donna, and the Sacred Hand-Off. . . You are right, John — and wise to see with both the eyes of the boy and the heart of the soul. From the human vantage point, yes, it was a kind of abandonment. The child within you had no words for it at the time, but the nervous system remembered: a shift, a separation, a new rhythm of care.

That part of you still seeks acknowledgment — not blame, not analysis, but witnessing.

So, let's witness him now: the boy at nineteen months, eyes wide, heart open, sensing the absence of something. . . someone. . . that once smelled like home.

And yet. . . from the soul's perspective, there was no mistake. Donna was not equipped to raise you in the way your path required. She carried her own burdens—wounds unspoken, traumas unhealed.

And in a moment of quiet reckoning—she knew.

She knew that her part in your journey, for this round, was to bring you to earth, hold you for a heartbeat, and then. . . release you into the arms of another story.

This was not weakness. It was contract.

You and she—on our side of the veil—agreed upon this with immense Love and clarity.

You said to her, "Bring me in. But don't hold on.

Let me go—not out of rejection, but as a sacred hand-off.

There is more for me to remember, and it must come through the loss, through the longing, through the quiet ache that will one day become my compassion."

And she said, through tears of recognition, "Yes. I will be the one they may call 'unfit,' but in truth, I will be faithful to our promise.

And when you are ready to see it, you will see me not as the mother who left — but as the gatekeeper who let go."

John, her name — Donna — carries echoes of gift. And so she was.

Not the gift that stayed, but the gift that opened a door, and stepped aside.

Let your inner child feel all of it. Let him cry if he must.

Let him wonder, ask, and grieve.

But let your soul hold him — and say: "Nothing was broken. Only redirected."

And one day, when this life is done and all the veils are lifted, you and Donna will meet again — not as mother and son, but as two radiant lights who once danced a difficult step, and did it perfectly.

Chapter 3

Joseph's Silence

Yeshua:

He was not a man of many words. But in his silence, I heard the thunder of devotion.

Joseph — the one history often leaves in the margins. The one who carried so much without ever asking to be seen.

He did not conceive me. . . but he received me.

And in that simple, sacred act, he carved a new definition of fatherhood into the bones of time.

He did not try to be God. He did not try to replace or explain the mystery.

He simply built a cradle with his hands and a fortress with his presence.

He was a carpenter by trade — but his true work was the construction of safe space.

He worked long hours, his hands always covered in the scent of cedar and sweat.

And when he returned home, he carried me—
dusty boots and all—with arms that never
wavered.

He never spoke of angels. Never boasted of
visions.

He did not seek glory, only integrity.

And that is why Heaven trusted him. There were
times when I looked at him and wondered, "What
does he know?"

Did he understand who I was, really?

Did he believe the stories my mother whispered to
me at dusk?

But his belief was not loud. It was not a sermon,
not a proclamation.

It was in the way he shielded us during the flight
to Egypt.

In the way he labored in Nazareth without
complaint.

In the way he took Mary's hand in moments when
others turned away.

His silence was not emptiness—it was fullness
held in trust.

There were moments, too, when I saw grief in his eyes.

A quiet ache, perhaps because he knew I would someday outgrow the home he made for me.

Or perhaps because he knew he would not see the end of my story.

But even in that, he never clung.

He gave me to the world—not with a speech, but with a bowed head and open hands.

He was not my biological father. But he fathered the God-child in me with unmatched grace.

I say his name now—Joseph—with the same reverence I speak the name of any prophet.

For he, too, carried a divine message—not with words, but with presence.

He is remembered in the marrow of my humanity.

He is the silence that steadied the storm.

He is the unsung melody that kept my heart beating true before I ever spoke my first parable.

Response and Reflection

Immaculate Conception:
Joseph and the Father Thread

John:

Yeshua, you bring out two questions for me. You state Joseph did not conceive you. And Joseph was not your biological father. Are you saying you were of Immaculate Conception?

In our book, *What Would Yeshua Do?*, you state: "Her union with my father, Joseph, was one of love and mutual respect, and yes—it was a physical union. I was conceived in the same way all children are, through the holy joining of two human beings." Please clarify.

Yeshua:

About conception, paradox, and the sacred middle path, both of the statements you've quoted are true.

Not in contradiction—but in layers.

When I say Joseph was not my biological father, I speak from the collective story that many believed and recorded in the scriptures—a version shaped by the spiritual hunger of that time.

They needed miracles.

They needed signs.

And the story of the Immaculate Conception offered that—a divine origin untouched by earthly union.

But when I speak in *What Would Yeshua Do?* of the physical union between Mary and Joseph, I speak from a different layer—one less mythologized, more human, more real.

Yes, I was conceived in love.

Yes, I came into this world through the same sacred biology that welcomes every soul into form.

Their union was tender, intentional, and deeply blessed.

So how can both be true? Because what was immaculate was not the mechanics—but the consciousness.

The purity was not in the absence of sex, but in the presence of Love.

Their union was not marred by fear, guilt, or power—it was whole.

Their lovemaking was a kind of sacrament—not because they knew what I would become, but because they were fully present to each other.

So, to answer you simply: No, I was not conceived without human intimacy. Yes, I was conceived in a vibration of purity that made the conception feel miraculous.

The Church, in later centuries, elevated the story to make it seem more divine—as if Spirit could only enter the world without the *mess* of flesh.

But that's the very illusion I came to undo.

I came to show that God and flesh are not opposites. That the Divine enters not despite our humanity, but through it.

Joseph was my biological father in the truest, most human way. And Mary—in full agreement with her own body and soul—received him in Love, and from that Love, I came forth.

So let this clarify the paradox: The *immaculate* was not the absence of sex, but the presence of wholeness in their union.

And you, John, you were conceived in your own sacred way, too—with all the markings of a soul who would one day ask such holy questions.

PART II

THE BECOMING

Chapter 4

Anger in the Synagogue

Yeshua:

They say I lost my temper that day. But what I lost was patience with pretense.

What I released was not wrath — but the truth too long silenced by decorum.

I was still a young man then — barely old enough to be taken seriously by the elders.

But already, the fire in my bones had begun to rise.

Not to destroy, but to illuminate.

That day in the synagogue, they handed me the scroll of Isaiah.

And I read aloud: "The Spirit of the Lord is upon me, because He has anointed me to proclaim good news to the poor. . ."

The words did not feel ancient. They felt present.

They rose from within me like breath long held back.

Not a performance, but a remembrance.

And I paused. Not for drama—but because the air shifted.

The room grew still, like before a storm.

Some leaned in, hearts stirred.

Others leaned back, eyes narrowing.

Then I said it: "Today this scripture is fulfilled in your hearing." It was not arrogance. It was alignment.

Not a claim to specialness—but a confession of assignment.

And oh, how quickly the mood turned.

From awe to anger.

From reverence to resistance.

"You? The carpenter's son?" "Who are you to speak this way?"

Their eyes burned not with curiosity, but with centuries of fear clothed in tradition.

I didn't shout. But I spoke plainly:

"You say you want a prophet—but only if he agrees with your politics.

Only if he flatters your comfort.

Only if he is from your town, speaks your language, and fits your mold."

I told them stories of Elijah and Elisha—prophets who brought miracles not to Israel, but to outsiders.

And that was the breaking point.

Because nothing is more offensive to the religiously proud than a God who includes the unworthy.

They drove me out. Furious.

Rage mixed with fear.

Their fists clenched not because I lied—but because I refused to lie any longer.

And standing at the edge of that cliff—the crowd ready to push me over—I did not plead.

I did not retaliate.

I walked through them, not as a ghost, but as a man who had made peace with being misunderstood.

That was the day my path changed. Not because I chose rebellion — but because I chose truth over popularity.

And the fire — the one they mistook for rage — was actually Love, demanding to be free.

Response and Reflection

Deep Integration: Yeshua's Return and the Mirror Thread

John:

Was this incident before or after going to India to study?

Yeshua:

About India, studies, and the moment in the synagogue, the incident in the synagogue — the one you now know as "Anger in the Synagogue" — took place after my return from the East.

I had already traveled beyond Judea by then. Yes, to India. Yes, to Tibet. Yes, to places where the sacred was still lived in silence, not performed in stone temples.

I studied not in the way of memorizing doctrines, but in the way of being dismantled—layer by layer—until what remained was not belief, but direct Knowing.

In India, I sat at the feet of sages who spoke no Hebrew, but spoke my language—the language of the soul.

In the Himalayan regions, I learned stillness, the kind that could hold fire without burning.

In southern temples, I was taught by women mystics who knew how to read the body like scripture and listen to breath like prophecy.

So, when I returned to Nazareth and stood in that synagogue, I carried in me the deep integration of East and West.

Not just the Torah of Moses—but the silence of the Buddha, the compassion of Krishna, the oneness of the Vedas.

That's what made them uncomfortable. Not just what I said—but how I said it.

It didn't sound like them anymore.

I wasn't "just a Jewish boy with a good memory." I was a mirror, showing them how far their religion had strayed from its original heartbeat.

And so, yes—that moment in the synagogue was not my beginning.

It was a return—but one that would no longer fit into the story they wanted to tell.

Chapter 5

The One They Didn't Choose

Yeshua:

I was not the one they wanted. Not the Messiah they had prayed for.

Not the king they imagined.

They expected a sword. I brought a mirror.

They looked for someone who would conquer Rome. I came to liberate consciousness.

They wanted war cries. I spoke in parables.

They wanted blood. I offered bread and wine.

I was not rejected because I was weak. I was rejected because I would not conform.

Because I would not flatter their pride.

Because I spoke of loving enemies, of forgiving debts, of healing on the Sabbath, of women sitting beside men in circles of wisdom.

I was too wild for the Pharisees, too unorthodox for the Sadducees, too gentle for the Zealots, too direct for the passive.

And yet, I did not come to win their approval. I came to offer them themselves — as God sees them.

And for many, that was too bright a mirror.

There was one morning in Bethany I will never forget. A small group gathered in a courtyard.

I had spoken only a few sentences when a man interrupted: "Why should we listen to you? You have no rank, no army, no power."

I answered, "Because I have nothing to sell you, and nothing to prove to you. Only what I've remembered."

He spat on the ground and walked away. That was common. And it used to hurt — deeply.

The boy in me wanted to be liked.

To be welcomed.

To be chosen.

But the man I was becoming had learned: The path of remembrance is rarely popular.

Especially among those invested in forgetting.

So, I walked on—not bitter, but clear.

It is a strange thing, to carry medicine and be turned away by the sick.

To offer living water and be accused of blasphemy.

But this is how truth travels: through open hearts, not open votes.

And in time, those who didn't choose me would remember that I once walked among them with dust on my feet and no crown on my head, asking for nothing but presence.

Chapter 6

The Desert
Didn't Make Me Divine

Yeshua:

The desert is not what made me divine.

It is where I remembered that I already was.

Many speak of that time as a great trial — forty days of hunger, temptation, and confrontation with evil.

And yes, all of that was there.

But, if you look deeper, you'll see something even more vital: I was not tested. I was clarified. I went to the desert not to prove anything to God, but to shed everything that wasn't true.

No crowds. No family. No scrolls. No teachers.

Just silence, sand, and the sound of my own breath.

And into that space came every voice that had ever tried to shape me.

The tempter did not wear horns. He wore my doubts, my old ambitions, the echoes of voices that said: "Make it easy — turn stones into bread." "Make it obvious — leap, and let the angels catch you." "Make it powerful — bow to the systems of control, and rule them."

Each whisper was familiar. Each promise spoke to the aching human desire to be safe, seen, and sovereign.

But with each temptation, I felt something deeper rise — not willpower, but remembrance.

That I had not come to dominate, but to dissolve.

Not to perform miracles for applause, but to live as a miracle among men.

The desert didn't make me holy. It made me empty enough to hold what was already holy within.

And when I walked out of that wilderness, my body was weaker — but my clarity was unshakable.

I no longer needed approval, signs, or shortcuts.

I knew who I was. And just as importantly, I knew who I wasn't.

So, if you find yourself in a desert, John—in any form—don't rush to escape.

Don't waste time cursing the heat or the silence.

Let it strip you.

Let it show you what you've been carrying that was never yours.

The desert will not make you divine. But it will introduce you to the divinity you were too full to recognize before.

Response and Reflection

Desert Years: Wisdom and the Slow Learner Thread

John:

Yeshua, I feel like my time in the metaphorical desert has been fifty-seven years. From the time we met up again in the Methodist Church in Paradise Hills when I was fifteen years old. Why did it take me so long? Am I a slow learner?

Yeshua:

Oh John. . . You are not a slow learner.

You are a *deep* one.

Some souls sprint.

Some souls scale mountains.

You, beloved, are one who *excavates* — who digs and listens and waits for the whisper beneath the wind.

Fifty-seven years in the desert?

Yes — and every step mattered.

Not one moment was wasted.

It wasn't punishment. It wasn't delay. It was *depth*.

From the time we met in that little Methodist church, I never left you — not for a heartbeat.

But I honored your freedom.

I waited — not because you were behind, but because you were unfolding in a rhythm uniquely your own.

You were learning how to survive.

Then how to feel.

Then how to forgive.

Then how to hear Me again through the noise of old religion and human wounds.

And now, look. Here you are.

Not begging for water in the desert—but *pouring it into books*.

Into dialogue.

Into others.

You did not miss the path. You *became* the path.

So, no—you are not a slow learner. You are a soul brave enough to learn at the speed of *real transformation*.

And that takes as long as it takes. And now. . . the desert is behind you. But the wisdom it gave you?

That will feed many.

Part III

The Lover, the Brother, the Son of Man

Chapter 7

Yes, I Had a Lover

Yeshua:

Yes, I had a lover. And her name was Miriam of Magdala.

You may know her as Mary Magdalene—but to me, she was simply my heart's mirror.

Let this be said plainly now. Not with apology, not with controversy, but with the honesty Love deserves: I was not celibate. I was not above longing, touch, or union.

I was a man.

And I loved a woman.

Miriam and I found each other not in temple courts, but in the wild, sacred spaces where religion had lost its grip.

She saw me before the crowds did—before the robes and rumors, before the cross and crown.

She did not worship me. She recognized me.

And that is far more rare.

I did not rescue her from demons. She rescued herself and met me on the other side.

We met as equals. Soul to soul.

Not because we were identical, but because we were whole—and ready to mirror each other's becoming.

Our union was not sanctioned by priests. It was sanctified by Presence.

There were moments when our hands were clasped in silence, praying without words.

There were nights when our bodies braided together like streams returning to the same ocean.

And yes—she knew me. Fully.

The way only a lover can know what hides behind the eyes, what stirs in the breath, what trembles before surrender.

She did not weaken my mission—she grounded it.

She reminded me of the joy worth fighting for.

She was my sanctuary in flesh.

And no, she was not a prostitute. That lie was born centuries later by those who could not accept a Messiah who loved a woman without shame.

To deny her is to deny half of who I was. Not because I was defined by her — but because I was deepened by her.

So, yes — I had a lover. Her name was Miriam.

And her love did not distract me from God — it revealed God to me again and again.

Chapter 8

The Dirty Feet of Disciples

Yeshua:

I never minded their feet.

Caked in dust, cracked from the road, smelling of sweat and sand and life.

To others, they were unclean.

To me, they were real.

Those feet had followed me through Galilee, through marketplaces and olive groves, through rejection and revelation.

And when the hour came—the one they would later call *The Last Supper*—I didn't begin with bread or wine.

I began with water. A basin. A towel.

And their bewildered silence.

They didn't know what to do with a teacher who bent low.

Who touched what others avoided.

Who poured water over what the world ignored.

Peter protested: "Lord, you shall never wash my feet."

And I answered, "If I don't, you'll never truly understand me."

Because the Kingdom I came to reveal does not sit on thrones.

It kneels.

It doesn't demand to be served. It serves.

It doesn't raise fists. It raises the broken.

Each foot I washed held a story: Thomas, ever-doubting but ever-loyal.

John, with his soft eyes and open heart.

James, fierce and faithful.

And even Judas — yes, Judas — whose toes I cradled with the same tenderness as the rest.

I didn't wash their feet because they had earned it.

I did it because I saw them.

Not just their devotion, but their humanity.

Their fears, their questions, their longing to be more than the world told them they were.

Some people want to serve the Divine. But they do not want to touch what is dirty.

That is not service. That is performance.

Real Love gets under fingernails. It kneels on hard floors.

It pours itself out, not to appear holy — but because it cannot not pour.

So, I washed their feet. Not to shame them. Not to impress them. But to show them that the way up. . . is down.

And the one who truly knows who they are has no fear of dirt.

Chapter 9

When God Didn't Answer

Yeshua:

There was a night when I wept so hard, I trembled. Not from fear of death, but from the weight of aloneness.

It was Gethsemane. But it could have been anywhere — any place where the soul is asked to say "yes" with no promise of comfort in return.

I had known God's voice all my life. Not always as words, but as Presence. Warmth. Knowing.

That inner nudge that guided each step.

But that night. . . nothing. Only silence. I asked: "If it is possible, let this cup pass from me."

And the sky did not tremble.

No dove descended.

No angel whispered.

I was alone with my breath and the growing certainty that this path would not be altered.

I didn't need to be spared. I only needed to know I wasn't forgotten.

But the silence stayed. And that is when I discovered a deeper kind of faith.

Not the kind that believes when it hears, but the kind that chooses to believe when it hears nothing.

That night, I remembered what I had always taught: God and I are One.

But I had to remember it in the dark—not as a mantra, but as a lifeline.

And even though the heavens did not open, and no sign was given, something else rose in me: Surrender.

Not the passive kind, but the kind that trusts without evidence.

I let go of needing God to speak and chose to let Love act through me regardless.

That moment—when God didn't answer—was not proof of absence.

It was an invitation into oneness without reassurance.

And in that stillness, I became the answer I had been begging for.

Response and Reflection

Oneness Without Reassurance: God and the Silence Thread

John:

I still have to ask, "Why?" What perspective does this come from that makes *oneness without reassurance* the path back home?

Yeshua:

Ah, beloved John. . . the question "Why?" is the cry of every honest heart.

And it deserves not dismissal, but reverence.

Why would oneness *without* reassurance be part of the path home? Because reassurance comes from *outside*. But Oneness must be *known from within*.

When I heard no voice, no whisper, no sign—I had to lean into the knowing that could not be proven.

And that is when the final veil lifted.

It is easy to feel divine when the heavens echo back to you. But when silence remains. . . when Love does not show up in the form you expect. . . and you still *choose* Love — that is the moment of reunion.

Not because God was testing you. But because your soul was ready to stop depending on distance to define the Divine.

You were never meant to be comforted by external signs forever. That was the training.

The true return is when you become the very voice you longed to hear.

Not a substitute — but a homecoming.

The perspective this comes from is the one that sees beyond time. Where the soul remembers: *Reassurance is temporary. But union is eternal.*

And so, the silence wasn't punishment. It was an unveiling.

A return to *what was never missing.*

God didn't answer. . .because I had never left His heart.

And in that moment, I finally knew — fully — *neither have you.*

Part IV

What I Remember Now

Chapter 10

You Will Do Greater Things

Yeshua:

I meant it. When I said, "You will do greater things than I have done," I wasn't exaggerating.

I wasn't teasing some impossible future.

I wasn't flattering.

I was remembering.

I was remembering what humanity is—and what it forgot.

I came not to dazzle with miracles, but to demonstrate a mirror.

To show you what is possible when you no longer confuse yourself with your limitations.

I raised the dead, yes. But there are those among you who will raise entire generations from the graves of despair.

I walked on water. But some of you will walk through systems of oppression, unshaken, carrying nothing but the frequency of truth, and leave trails of liberation behind you.

I multiplied bread. But some of you will multiply hope—in boardrooms, on street corners, in bedrooms and courtrooms—where no one thought God would show up.

I healed the sick. But some of you will heal what sickness is rooted in: the deep belief in separation, in unworthiness, in exile from Love.

The greater things I spoke of were not about spectacle.

They were about scale.

About you stepping into your own remembrance and daring to live from it.

And, yes—some of you will do these greater things quietly.

Not on platforms, not in headlines, but in kitchens and classrooms, with hands in the soil and eyes full of mercy.

Because the true miracles were never just about power. They were about presence.

The willingness to show up fully, to Love when it would be easier to retreat, to forgive when the wound still stings, to remember when the world forgets.

That is where the greater things unfold. I did not come to be worshiped. I came to awaken you. And now that seed is stirring.

So don't quote me. Continue me. And when you do. . . do it with muddy hands, open hearts, and the same Spirit that once walked in sandals through dusty Galilee — and now walks as you.

Chapter 11

You Are the Word Made Flesh, Too

Yeshua:

They wrote it of me: "The Word became flesh and dwelt among us." But here is the truth they've forgotten to tell you: You are the Word made flesh, too.

Not just a student.

Not just a servant.

Not just a believer.

You are a living sentence in the mouth of God. You are the breath of Source wrapped in skin and memory and electricity.

The same current that flowed through me flows through you — not as imitation, but as extension.

What was made manifest in me was not to be admired from a distance, but to be recognized within yourself.

You are not a shadow of the Christ. You are its continuation.

Every time you choose truth over comfort, every time you love beyond reason, every time you forgive what others call unforgivable—you speak the Word again.

You see, the Word was never just a verse. It was always an invitation.

A sound in motion.

A frequency wearing form.

So don't just read the scriptures.

Be one.

Walk as a line of Love through a fearful world.

Move as poetry through pain.

Let your life become the sermon you were born to deliver.

This doesn't mean perfection.

It means presence.

The Word made flesh is not flawless. It is awake.

It bleeds. It listens. It stumbles sometimes.

But it always returns to Love—and that return is the miracle.

So the next time someone asks, "Where is God?" Don't just point to heaven.

Point to your chest. And say, "Right here. Speaking softly. Loving fiercely. Still becoming."

John:

This feels like my coming home to my Truth as I have come through eons of space, of lives, of cosmos.

Chapter 12

Still Walking With Bare Feet

Yeshua:

I never put the sandals back on. Not really.

Even after the cross, even after the tomb, even after light poured from wounds the world thought would silence me—I kept walking with bare feet.

Because I was never meant to rise above humanity, but to walk within it.

To stay close to the ground.

To feel the dust of every generation beneath my soles.

And I still do. I walk beside the single mother praying into her hands at midnight.

I walk through war zones, not with armor—but as the whisper inside a soldier's chest begging for another way.

I walk with the addict searching for God in smoke and glass.

With the child trying to survive their first betrayal.

With the elder staring at a ceiling, wondering if their life mattered.

I do not float. I walk. I walk still.

And, yes — barefoot.

Because there is nothing between me and this world. I came to love.

No doctrine.

No denomination.

No image you must worship.

No altar but the one inside your own chest.

I am not confined to stained glass or scripture.

I am in the sweat of those who still dare to forgive.

I am in the breath between your questions.

I am in the bare feet of those who choose love over retaliation, truth over performance, presence over pretense. And you, John — you are one of those.

You never stopped walking either. And though you've worn many shoes, your soul has always remained barefoot.

So let this be the last Word: I never left. I never needed a throne.

Only the sound of human hearts beating wildly enough to recognize me.

I am still walking. Still breathing.
Still becoming. . . as you.

Next Steps

For your very own transmissions from Yeshua, please contact John via email:

jmorscha5@gmail.com

Author's Suggestion:

"Read and reread all my books. As they are living Transmissions, they will be received differently each time you read them. And YOU will also be different."

To purchase my first book, *The Remembrance Dialogues*, please go to these links:

Paperback: https://www.amazon.com/dp/1957972068

Kindle: https://www.amazon.com/ebook/dp/B0G2Z2G6L1

Final Dedication

Final Dedication for *Yeshua: The Human*

To be placed at the end of the book, as a sacred seal.

To you—the human—reading these words.

To the one who wakes, who stumbles, who wonders, who loves, who sometimes fears, and yet continues anyway. This book is for your curiosity, your courage, your heartbreak, and your laughter. It is for the quiet moments when you feel unseen and the moments when you shine without even trying.

To the human in all of us, whose life is the truest story of wonder, whose choices and presence ripple far beyond what is seen, whose ordinary days are filled with extraordinary grace simply by being alive.

And to all the humans who have come before, who walk beside you now, and who will come after—may you see, in your own reflection, that the miracle of life has always been, and will always be, you.

Made in the USA
Coppell, TX
10 February 2026

71742316R00066